MIRRAN THOUGHT

MIRRAN THOUGHT

Spitzwiesenstr. 50
90765 Fürth
Germany

www.dwmirran.de
www.empty.de
empty@empty.de

READ TWENTYSEVEN
(MT-639)

Printed and Published by:
BoD - Books on Demand, Norderstedt
www.bod.de
info@bod.de

ISBN: 9783754371893

First printing 2021

MIRRAN THOUGHT is the publishing arm of
Mirran Threat, a company devoted to releasing the
music and writings of the various members of Doc
Wör Mirran. Mirran Thought and Mirran Threat are
both divisions of MT Undertainment.

The
Matala Son

Joseph B. Raimond

Written and drawn in Matala, Crete, Greece, September 1 to 12, 2021

Edited in Fürth, Germany

As always, in loving memory of Frank Abendroth and Tom Murphy.

For Conny, my perfect angel

Dedicated to Kai, Franky and of course Matala George

Cover art by Joseph B. Raimond "Matala Model" September 10th, 2021 Matala, Greece

Back cover photo by Conny Eirich
Page 60 photo by Judith Weber

This is DWM release Nr. 191

Schmoe Joe

I am
This ever changing blob
I can fit in almost everywhere
Everywhere, that is
Except your square
Preconceptions
Of what I am, should be
Or what I once was

The truth is
I have never fit in
Even back then,
When I was stupid enough
To actually want to

It has taken a lifetime
For me to realize
That it is okay not to be
A square
I have learnt to accept
Who I am

But can you?
Either buy me another beer,
Or get lost

Birds

suddenly,
the robbery bird dropped
into attack mode
zoomed through the flock
of panic stricken
sing birds,
sixteen of which
splattered their life blood
in panic
across the windshields
of oncoming traffic

they aint
signin' no mo'!

Matala Shpongled

the sun is hot
the beer is cold
so I am adequately equipped
everything is fine
as I sit in the shade
watching the deep blue waves
crash onto the rocks
near the Roman graves
I sip my beer, try to write
pretend I am a happy
and listen to my Shpongle

3 / 4

The way I figure it
If I'm lucky
I'm about three quarters
Of the way
Through this circus ride
And what a wild ride
It's been!

I've been through it all:
Car accidents, a tornado
A hurricane and an earthquake
I witnessed and survived
A jihadist terrorist attack

Good friends & a bad marriage
I had a record in the charts
I put out my own music on vinyl
(it don't get cooler than that!)

I stood on a stage
And watched fans sing along
To lyrics that I wrote!

I have shown my paintings
In Paris and in San Francisco
I have published my own books
(like this one!)

I watched my two beautiful children
Grow up

And, after ¾ of a lifetime looking
I finally found
The love of the most beautiful woman
In the world

Right now,
Sitting at a small table
With a cold beer, paper and a pen
Looking out over the beautiful
Bay of Matala, Greece
What is quickly becoming
My second home
Watching the waves
(listening to Shpongle again!)
I can finally say,
At least for this one
Brief moment
That I know happiness

If Matala decides
To keep me forever
Maybe a heart attack on the beach
Or drowning in the bay
Please do not be sad
I have already lived

Enough for ten people

Simply print this poem
At the end of my last book
And move on

Because

Today is life,
Tomorrow never come(s)

 Kai

Goodbye,
Matala Kai
Both of us,
Little nobodies
In the grand machinery
That runs this corrupt world
The only real difference
Between us was
Maybe I got the better breaks

On the other hand
I got to envy you, for
You got to live in paradise

Now, suddenly,
You are gone!
And those few beers we shared
Were destined to be
Our last

But if I can
Still give you anything
Let it be this
Little poem
Just for you

Chick Pisser

These bikini cladded
Teenage chickens
Put on these long T-shirts
After leaving their sea swim
And the resulting
Wet spots
Look like lactating nipples
And pissed pants

The Heart Of The Art

call it beatnik
hippy or punk
or even techno
if you have to
but the heart of the art
is always the underground
for only there
do pennies create
timeless art

The 2nd Most Worst

thing,
Besides looking in a mirror
Is realizing
That whole years
Have zoomed by
And I cannot,
No matter how hard I try
Remember
A single thing
I did,
Said,
Or created
In that time

Listen To Charlie

Okay,
I try to be something
But I'll admit it
I'm usually nothing
But after all these years
At least I still try
And I have learned
Deep down
Not to care anymore
What others think

At least
That is something

<u>Accomplish</u>

I know it is impossible
But still,

I want to be all the people
I want to be

I want all my dreams
Fulfilled

And even if I need five lifetimes,
To accomplish everything
I want to do,

I aint giving up!

Red Beach

Don't bother
Going to the red beach
The climb up is a bitch
And once there
All the ugly
Sagging will turn your stomach

All those gravity damaged
Boobs and balls
Will give you nightmares
For a week

And,
You still have to climb
Back!

I Love Rock & Roll

Nicky brought me to Zappa
Tom got me into Neil Young
Bernard showed me The Doors
My uncle Klaus
Bought me my first Beatles album
Pink Floyd brought Conny and I
Together
Conny and I together discovered
Shpongle

I love rock and roll

Broken Promises

First the hippies
With all their talk
Of free love, revolution
And smash the establishment
And where did it all lead?
Other than some timeless music,

Nowhere

Today, they vote Republican
Are more prude
And conservative
Than their square parents ever were

Fuck Woodstock
Altamont is their true legacy

Then came the dawn
Of the 90s
The fall of the wall
The splintering of the Soviet Union
The end of the cold war
We all thought that
Now we have nothing left
To fear

"Winds of change"
My ass!

Today, it's
Me! Me! Me!
Every man for himself
Everyone at everyone
Else's throats

And god forbid
If you believe
In gay rights
A woman's right to decide
About her own body
If you hate guns
Or criticize the good ol'
US of A

Sometimes
I feel like
The last man standing

Infinity

I have this fire
Inside me
But I still feel so cold
Like nothing really works
Like it should
And I am forever
Ugly

I am so tired of regrets
Afraid of broken promises
To myself
And unfulfilled dreams

Afraid death
Won't be the end

Self-Help

I'm always either
Regretting the past
Or dreaming
Of the future

I only live in the moment
When I'm asleep

34

A Matala Day

The morning waves
Push the pebbles to the beach
Only to annoy me
As the little stones
Are destined for the
Inside my shoe

The village buildings
Still offer shade
On the hottest of days
But that relentless old sun
Is already planning
To sunburn my feet today

An army
Of overweight, faceless
Foreign tourists
(I'm one of them, I know!)
Begin their morning routines
Placing their towels
Strategically on the deck chairs
To mark their territory
Then go away
To breakfast

The afternoon saltwater
Is cold,
But refreshing

Until an annoying little fish
Keeps trying
To nibble on my feet

The evening brings gluttony
As we feast ourselves fat
At our favourite restaurant
With the best food
In the world

A raki
Nightcap
Completes our day

But it is hard to sleep
As our bed
Is full
Of sand

Travelling Home

That dingy 5th floor room
With no bathroom
And a smelly carpet
In that run-down building
In the Tenderloin
Of San Francisco

That beautiful hand-built
Wooden hut on a hillside
With a roaring waterfall
And crystal-clear stream
On the edge of town
In Fort William, Scotland

That little room in Prague
In that former whore house
Where we breakfasted
In the morning
Next to the stage
Where the naked girls
Once grinded against their poles

That compartment
We had all to ourselves
With all the coffee
We could drink
On the sleeper train
We took from Croatia

That cute little apartment
With all those cats outside
And a bar nearby
With unbelievably cheap
Beer and wine
Out on the outskirts
Of Barcelona, Catalonia

And that wonderful shack
Deep in the Arizona desert
With the downward slopping bed
And that horrible
Tomato flavored beer
We accidentally bought
In one stop-signed
Chloride, Arizona

Or that cheap smelly room
With a cockroach infested bathroom
And broken one-armed bandits
In the gaudy lobby
In Las Vegas, Arizona

In Stella's rooms
With motherly Stella
Taking such good care of us
In beautiful Split, Croatia

Or that horrible, damp
Flood damaged little house
We rented
With the moldy coffee
When we visited our friend
General Sherman
In Three Rivers,
Arizona

Or now, in our funny
Little apartment
With the sticking front door
And a cave as a bathroom
Here in paradise
Matala, Crete

All these wonderful places
Where hundreds have stayed before
And hundreds will stay
After we are gone

But as a citizen
Of this planet
All of them
For me,
Are still home

Invisible

A loner
Like an ugly, blind mole
I burrow under
Popular society

For I was never cool
And no one can ever
Remember me

And when I am around people
I never seem to know what to say
And I don't know how
To kiss ass
And I never get invited
To cool parties
I am
Invisible

Which, I kind of like
For then, I'm not distracted
And no one can waste my time
In my life's work
To find myself

<u>Los Alamitos</u>

A fuckin' long time ago
Forty-one years, to be exact
I was living with my born-again dad
And his second wife Susan
In a suburb of Los Angeles
An ugly shit-hole of a place
Called Los Alamitos

I hated
Every minute I lived there

We lived not far
From a military base
And the racetracks

When I was only sixteen
I got my driver's license
Driving around
Los Alamitos

And I seem to remember
Driving on the freeway one day
Towards Long Beach
Some ugly old fuck driving a BMW
Cut me off!

Now that I think of it
It might have been

Charles Bukowski
Returning from the racetrack

So you see,
It took a very long time
More than forty years
But now I can finally
Say something interesting
About my life
In Los Alamitos

Hard To Believe...

But less than fifteen years ago
At the age of 44
I finally got my hair cut
Hair that had grown
Down to my
Ugly, old
Ass

I had it cut
Not for any other reason
But simply because
I finally, after decades of nagging

By my mom
By my band
And finally,
By myself

I finally realized
I didn't look cool
Instead, I looked like
A wanna-be hippy
A dumb dreamer
Not to be taken seriously

Now,
Everyone says I look better
Some of my current friends,

Though
Laugh when I show them old pictures
Of me with that long hair

Me, I'm still not sure
(but that you know, is a different problem)

So now,
Here I sit in my
Beloved Matala
Not looking like a hippy at all
But like a wanna-be
Writer

Like Hemmingway
Who I never liked!

Sometimes,
You just can't win!

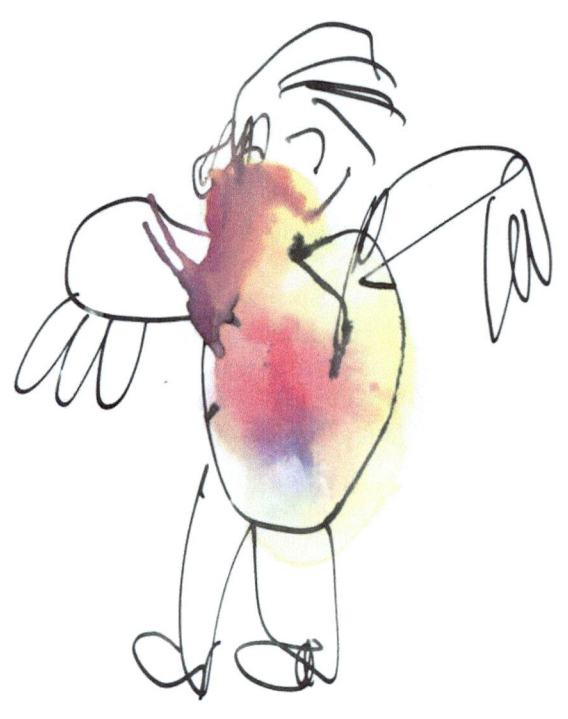

River

I'm too good at forcing
And not good enough
At flowing

I should be like
A lazy river
Here to enjoy the ride
I'll get somewhere
Eventually

So use me
Steer me
Where we need to go
Let me be your tool
And show me
That it is okay
Not always to be
Productive

Just as long
As I still
Get the credit

Poem For Me

From the very beginning
I never liked myself much
But considering
That what little self esteem
And self-respect
I had
Was beaten out of me
First by my dad
Then by my wife

By those that should
Have loved me

It is a wonder,
I am here at all

They used me
When it came in handy
Then discarded me
Like an empty beer bottle
Worthless, bothersome
Take out the trash, dammit!

Finally,
Everything I had
That meant something to me
Became worthless
In my fall

For decades, I had been falling
Losing little bits of me
On the way down

Then, I finally came
To the bottom of my well
There, the last thing I found
To cling to

Was hope

Hope saved me
From their "love"

But we all know
That falling down is easier
And faster
Than climbing up

But like a high-octane fuel
Hope helped me climb
Blistered and bleeding
Towards the light
The death of the ego
Where arrogance
Is meaningless
And no longer
In my vocabulary

And today,
Well, look at me!
Here I am!
Son of nature
Happy,
Writing nonsense
In the Matala sun

54

Erosion

Like the afternoon waves
That push the stones
To the sandy shore
I can feel the gloom coming
Pushing, thoughts
Of real or imagined
Illness
Eroding this fragile
Happiness

It was only a matter of time,
It always is
Before the storm of gloom
Sends me back
To the depths
I know so well

Soon,
Another life will pass
And my place in the queue
Keeps getting shorter

A Matala Sunset

As I listen
Carefully, intent
The sound
Of the waves
Is inspiring music
To my tinnitus inflicted ears

The colors of a sunset
More vivid
That any paintings
To my aging eyes

We lie on the beach
To watch the sun go down
Are witness
In this most magical of places
To the art
Of our mother, nature

In the most beautiful sunset
These eyes
Have ever seen

Fortune Teller

Foreboding
Believe it like
A palm reader
I somehow know, something bad
Is just around the corner

So, go ahead
Let's get it over with
Show your ugly,
Scarred face

Take it,
Snatch it, steal
Me from my love

Stop laughing!
I know I can't win!
But you can be damn sure,
That on my way down
I'll put up
A hell of a fight
Anyway

Joseph B. Raimond is an American expat living permanently in Germany. Besides his many writing and painting projects, he also has recorded dozens of albums under the collective name Doc Wör Mirran. He lives in Fürth, Germany.